RENEGADE CAR CAMPING

A GUIDE TO FREE CAMPSITES AND THE ULTIMATE ROAD TRIP EXPERIENCE

BRYAN SNYDER

LOST SOULS PUBLISHING, LTD.

Copyright © 2016 by Bryan Snyder

All rights reserved.

No part of this book may be reproduced in any form or by any electronic or mechanical means, including information storage and retrieval systems, without written permission from the author, except for the use of brief quotations in a book review.

ISBN 978-1-7348970-4-3

Cover photograph by Bryan Snyder

Interior photographs by Bryan Snyder, public domain or used by permission

Lost Souls Publishing, Ltd.

www.offthemapbooks.com

ALSO BY BRYAN SNYDER

Off The Map: Fifty-Five Weeks of Adventuring in the Great American Wilderness and Beyond

Further Off The Map: Fifty-Three Tales of Adventure along the Rougher Edges of American Wilderness

Falling Off The Map: Fifty-Four Explorations into the Wildest Reaches of the American West

Ten Renegade Camping Destinations: Free Public Camping Areas Big Enough to Fit You and a Dozen of Your Closest Friends

The Ghost and the Greyhound

CONTENTS

Introduction — vii

1. PUBLIC LANDS IN AMERICA — 1
   Federal Lands — 3
   National Forests — 4
   National Parks — 6
   BLM Lands — 8
   National Wildlife Refuges — 10
   National Recreation Areas — 12
   State Lands — 13
   County and Municipal Lands — 14

2. RENEGADE CAMPSITE HUNTING — 15
   A Drive into the Woods — 17
   Gathering Information — 20
   BLM Camping — 21
   Reservoirs — 22
   Private Timberlands — 23
   Abandoned Bridges and Roads — 24
   Town Parks — 25
   Power Lines and Cell Towers — 27
   Water Tanks and Towers — 29
   Hot Springs — 31

3. YOUR RENEGADE CAMPSITE — 34
   Vehicles — 35
   Tents — 36
   Vehicle Positioning — 39
   Bedding — 41
   Water Sources — 42
   Showering — 43
   Lighting — 45

Cooking	46
Shelter	47
Washing the Dishes	48
Seating	50
Toilet Training	52
Flat Tires, Dead Batteries	53
The Secret to Renegade Camping Peace-of-Mind	57
Leave No Trace	59
4. ROAD RESOURCES	62
The Loneliness Factor	63
Couchsurfing	65
Youth Hostels	68
AirBnB and Hipcamp	70
Hitchhiking	72
Rideshares	74
Backpacking	75
Free Campgrounds	77
Libraries	78
Smartphone Apps	80
Epilogue: The Road Goes Ever On	84
Links	87
Car Camping Equipment Checklist	89
About the Author	91
About the Vehicle	93

INTRODUCTION

Charlie was the best jeep a boy could have wanted. When the keys to this two-door, six-cylinder powerhouse fell into my hands twenty years ago, I had no idea how much endurance he possessed. 350,000 miles and countless adventures later, his blue paint is beginning to turn gray from sun damage, just as my own hairs are graying with age. But Charlie's engine remains strong, and he's eagerly anticipating our next expedition through the Rocky Mountain landscape.

Over the course of two decades, the two of us have learned several tricks regarding extended cross-country travel. This guide is designed to teach you many of our hard-earned techniques so that you can get out the door and experience the majestic expanses of North America with your own trusty vehicle. We want you to have the time of your life. We want you to have adventures so epic that your grandchildren will be telling their grandchildren about them. And we don't want you to go broke in the process of said adventures.

Of course, you're probably wondering how you can afford to travel for months at a time. First of all, you don't need a high-clearance colossus capable of crushing redwoods beneath your tires. And you don't need to sell the farm in order to finance your vacation. You just need to acquaint yourself with the activity known to some as "renegade car camping".

I've gone years without paying for a single campsite, and I've pitched my tent in places far more scenic and epic than anything I could have paid money for. It takes a renegade attitude and a bit of knowledge about public lands that Charlie and I are happy to provide.

In Part One of this book, we'll give a brief overview of federal, state and other public lands in the United States.

In Part Two, we'll outline the types of renegade campsites you're likely to discover on those lands and show you how to search them out.

In Part Three, we'll teach you how to make the most of your primitive campsites so that you feel like a king or queen despite the absence of a proper throne (or a working pit toilet).

And in Part Four, we'll share one last batch of resources and tips on how to stay thrifty when you're on the road and away from your campsite.

You'll notice there is no Part Five: My Favorite Secret Camping Spots. That's for a good reason. Listing these overlooked areas could cause them to be quickly destroyed through overuse. I've selected ten locations that could withstand some extra attention, however, and put them into a free guidebook that you can download at *offthemapbooks.com/freebook*. Once you begin finding these campsites on your own, I think you'll agree on the need for some secrecy, and besides, part of the fun of being a renegade camper lies in the thrill of campsite hunting.

I've never made significant money as an environmental educator, yet I'm consistently able to take three months off every year to travel the American West. I'd like to give you that freedom, and knowledge of renegade camping is the key. Granted, employers tend to frown on extended absences, but if you are in between jobs, your unsettled circumstances may turn out to be the opportunity of a lifetime. After all, what better way to figure out your next chapter than with an epic road trip?

So whether you're escaping for a weekend venture to a hot springs, taking a summer sabbatical with the whole family, or working out a mid-life crisis, you should find something in this guide to make your trips more affordable, functional and magical.

Are you ready? Charlie is idling just outside with a full tank of gas. What say we take a tour around the country?

ONE
PUBLIC LANDS IN AMERICA

Public lands are one of the greatest legacies that our country possesses. You remember the song, "America, The Beautiful"?

> "O beautiful for spacious skies,
> For amber waves of grain,
> For purple mountain majesties

Above the fruited plain!"

Well, for me, that speaks of the best part of the United States: the land itself. We are exceptionally fortunate that despite the pressures of industry, resource extraction and other private interests, our federal government has kept about 28% of its 2.27 billion acres of land in the public trust. That includes a whole lot of mountain majesties and spacious skies. Another 12% is owned and managed by states, counties and municipalities.

All this land has to be managed, and so we elect representatives who pass laws determining how these public spaces can be used. Various agencies are in charge of implementing these laws, and they have to balance the needs of loggers, miners, ranchers, recreational users and the environment. If you're reading this guide, you're probably a recreational user.

This section will get you up to speed on these agencies and on the public lands they manage so that you can take advantage of your rights as a U.S. citizen and recreate to the best of your ability. If you don't need the overview, feel free to pull ahead, and Charlie and I will meet you down the road for Part Two.

Federal Lands

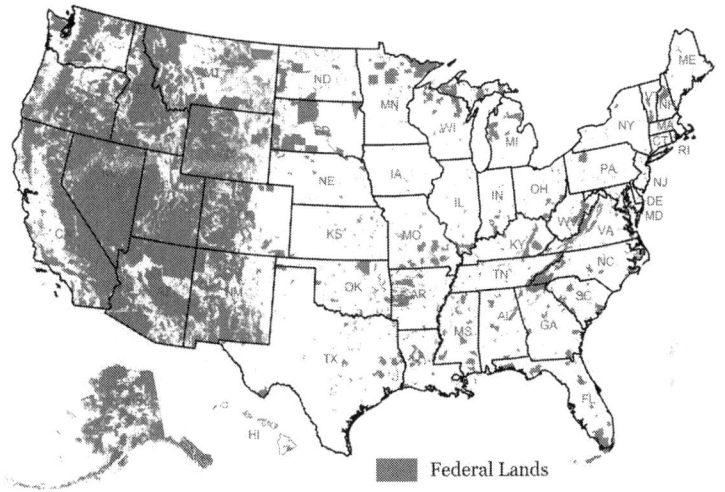

Federal Lands

Americans are lucky to live in a country where, at a certain point in its expansion, the government decided to stop giving away lands to private individuals, leaving a significant portion in the public trust to be managed by federal agencies. Not all agencies have the same mission, so it helps to look at the managers of federal lands individually; that way you can know what to expect when you're trying to scrounge up a campsite in their territory.

In the Department of Agriculture you will find the Forest Service, *because...* trees are like agricultural crops, right? Forest Service employees manage National Forests and National Grasslands, which makes them great allies for car campers to have.

In the Department of the Interior are multiple land managers, like the National Park Service (NPS), who oversee the National Parks as well as National Seashores, National Lakeshores, some

National Preserves, most National Monuments and numerous historic parks, sites, trails and battlefields. The Fish and Wildlife Service (FWS) manages the National Wildlife Refuge system. The Bureau of Reclamation oversees recreation areas around several of the dams and reservoirs that they manage. And the Bureau of Land Management (BLM) administers the remainder of the mostly unforested land, along with a few National Monuments.

The Department of Defense has large landholdings, including several campgrounds and recreation areas, but you are unlikely to gain permission to visit them unless you are active or retired military personnel.

Let's study the places these agencies manage one by one.

National Forests

Most of my most epic campsites have been found here. There are 155 National Forests, many of which were designated by President Teddy Roosevelt in a sneaky political maneuver that saved much of the landscapes of the Rockies, Cascades and Sierra Nevada mountain ranges from unbridled deforestation. The few National Forests east of the Mississippi were mostly cobbled together from failed farms that had been purchased by the federal government and replanted.

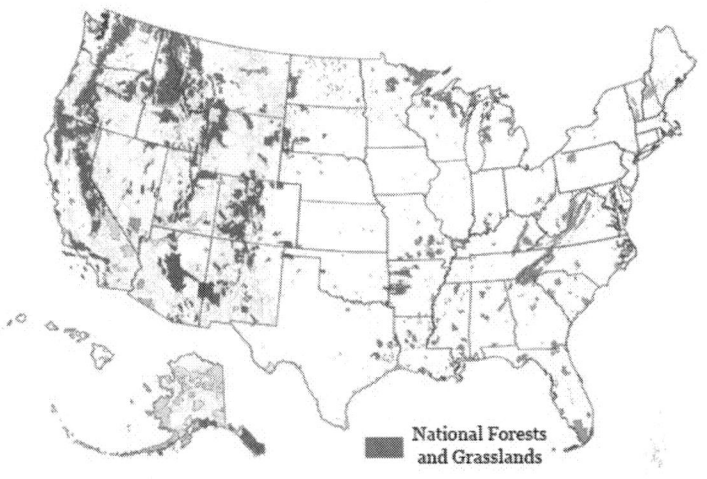

Unless otherwise posted, all National Forest and National Grassland areas are open to campsite seekers. Here's where you'll find great potential for renegade camping – also known by the less flashy term "dispersed camping". This simply means camping outside of established campgrounds. You may occasionally see "Camp Only In Designated Campsites" signs near National Parks and areas with potential for overuse, however. Popular forests have to be more carefully managed.

In National Forests, you can car-camp for 14 days in the same site. That's some pretty inexpensive lounging. Campgrounds will set you back $10-$20 a night, but there are a few free ones out there if you know where to look. More on that later.

National Parks

The National Park Service manages, as of 2015, 409 separate units, but normally just the big parks come to mind, like Yellowstone, the Grand Canyon and Yosemite. Should you see these places? Well, of course! It's practically your responsibility as an American! But it's hard to visit National Parks on the cheap.

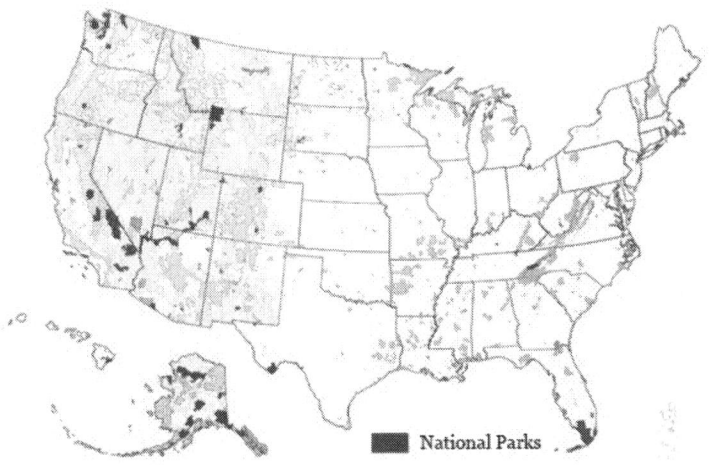

National Parks

Campgrounds will set you back about $20 a night, and the National Forests surrounding the Parks tend to have fewer opportunities for dispersed camping. Even when they do, it might not be worth the time it takes to leave the park every night; what you save in campground fees could be easily outweighed by gas expenditures. This is the only circumstance in which I will pay for camping, even though I absolutely hate doing it. Sometimes you just gotta remember that your time is valuable, too.

A couple of the lesser-known National Parks have free campgrounds hidden in hard-to-reach places. Some National Monuments feature free campgrounds and dispersed camping opportunities, especially the ones established by Presidential proclamation since 1996. These places were often carved out of existing National Forest or BLM lands and still retain their original Forest Service or BLM management.

BLM Lands

BLM lands get a bad rap because they typically include all the leftover lands in the United States that no one wanted to log, farm, homestead or preserve as a National Park or Forest. They contain 247 million acres of sagebrush or open desert – about one-eighth the total landmass of the whole country. 155 million acres have enough grass that ranchers will purchase permits to let their cattle graze there. And over 63,000 oil and gas wells have been drilled on these lands. These activities lead critics to suggest that BLM stands not for "Bureau of Land Management" but for "Bureau of Livestock and Mining". The agency's reputation for supporting extractive industries is definitely well-deserved, although recreation has been given more and more attention in recent decades.

RENEGADE CAR CAMPING 9

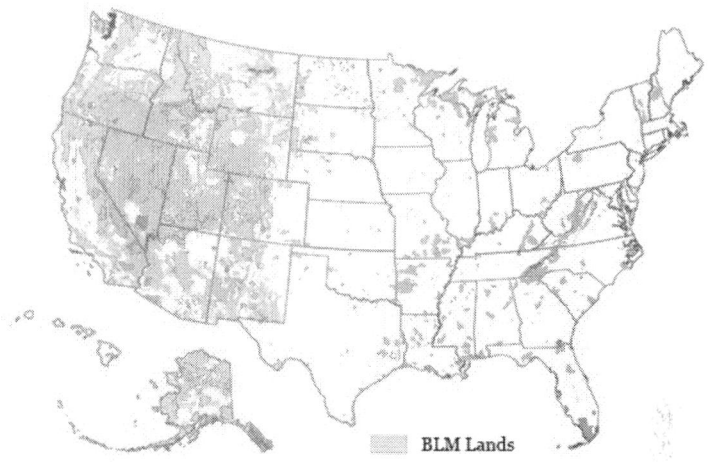

BLM Lands

Because BLM territory is so often overlooked by the typical American, it can provide tremendous opportunities for the renegade traveler. So many of the gorgeous, colorful badland landscapes of Utah, if not already incorporated into National Parks, lie on BLM land. Wide-open vistas abound. Dispersed camping is frequently easy; there is a 21-day limit before you need to migrate to a new spot. If you'd like to hole up for a longer period, Arizona and California have Long Term Visitor Areas where you can park a tent, car, van or RV for months at a time.

Like the ranger stations of the National Park Service and Forest Service, the BLM have their own information centers where you can gather intelligence on hikes, road conditions and campgrounds. If you're looking for free campgrounds, the BLM has a greater percentage than the other agencies, for certain.

National Wildlife Refuges

Teddy Roosevelt designated the first wildlife refuge in 1903, and today there are about 560 refuges covering over 150 million acres of land. The mission of the Fish and Wildlife Service is to conserve fish, wildlife and plant populations, but initially, animals were protected so that they could continue to be hunted by sportsmen. Preservation of ecosystems is a greater focus today, although hunting traditions have continued. If you visit a refuge, be prepared to make friends with hunters and wear bright clothing.

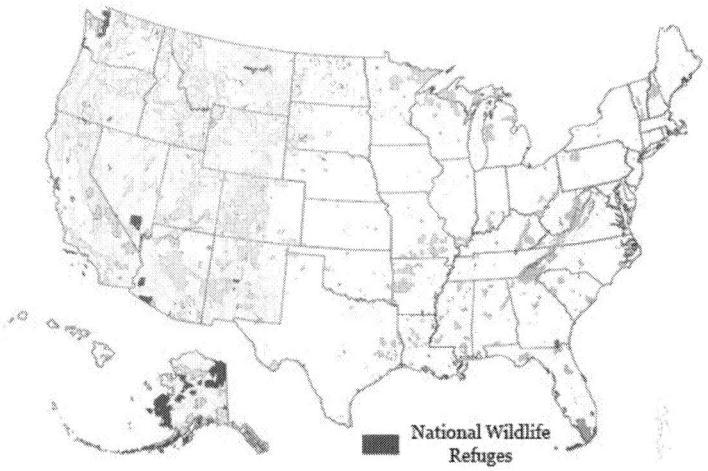

Dispersed camping opportunities are less prevalent, as refuges tend to have fewer roads open to the public. Free and pay-to-stay campgrounds occur in about the same proportions as they do in National Forests or BLM lands. To find the free ones, visit the refuge headquarters or look up the refuge online.

If you're thinking of checking these places out, bring binoculars and try taking a stroll at dawn. Or bring fishing gear, and you might be able to catch your own breakfast.

National Recreation Areas

Unlike the multiple-use mandates of the Forest Service and BLM, National Recreation Areas are managed, well, for outdoor recreation primarily. Many of the 44 NRAs were established in the aftermath of huge Army Corps of Engineers dam and reservoir projects – part of the great "Taming of the West".

If you're looking for cheap or free camping, NRAs with reservoirs will sometimes give you options. The NRAs that operate like urban parks, on the other hand, like Golden Gate NRA, are too close to large population centers to allow dispersed or free camping. The land would deteriorate from too much attention. Finding free camping near major cities is possibly the greatest challenge for the renegade camper, which is why I recommend Couchsurfing as an alternative in Part Four of this book.

State Lands

Just like the federal government, states have their own parks, forests, wildlife refuges and recreation areas. State parks typically have higher campground fees than federal parks - $35 a night at some parks in California. The higher fees may exist because states cannot run year-to-year budget deficits, unlike the federal government. Free state-run campgrounds, therefore, are a rarity.

This goes for state forests as well. Dispersed camping in state forests, however, is usually allowed.

County and Municipal Lands

Yep. Counties also can have their own parks, forests and refuges. And fortunately for the traveler, counties occasionally make their campgrounds free of charge because the visitors who stay there contribute to the local tourist economy.

Small towns sometimes allow free camping in their town parks for the same beneficial reason, and we'll revisit this topic in Part Two. Other public lands managed by towns and cities may be used for their water or electrical infrastructure. If you see metal fences, razor wire and "No Trespassing" signs, you may want to look for another place to camp, even if the land *is* technically part of the public domain.

TWO
RENEGADE CAMPSITE HUNTING

Here's where we take a leap of faith, people. Renegade camping. This is how I make extended summer travels possible on a limited budget. Hop into your vehicle of choice and head off into the public lands, driving onwards and upwards until you find a campsite tucked into the trees. Maybe there will be a gently bubbling stream nearby. Maybe you will have climbed to a beautiful vista where you can watch the sunset as you prepare an evening meal. Maybe there will be a hot springs within walking distance, and you can soothe your muscles and warm your bones before crawling into the tent for the night.

I gravitate towards dispersed camping because I love peace and solitude and because some of my greatest experiences with scenery and wildlife have happened at campsites in the middle of nowhere. Established campgrounds can be noisy, crowded, and can defeat the purpose of going into nature. You can't see the mountains if you're staring into the back of someone's RV, and you're not going to hear a pack of wolves howling if all you can hear is the sound of your neighbor's generator. If you've got a large family in tow, campgrounds are a tremendous convenience. But if it's just you and your partner... ditch the KOA and head for the hills.

I'll admit there are some downsides when you give up the amenities that campgrounds provide. Instead of a flush toilet or outhouse, you have to poop in the woods. Instead of water spigots, you have to bring your own water supply or filter water from streams. Instead of picnic tables, you have a bunch of flat rocks for a kitchen. And instead of a fire pit, you have a fire ring... but at least you can gather your own firewood. We'll discuss ways to be resourceful and how to mitigate the inconveniences in a later chapter. It's well worth it... don't be discouraged!

Charlie and I have worked as a team for so long that dispersed camping is second nature for us. I've honed my eye to spot the most obscure campsite locations, and Charlie uses his moderately high-clearance capabilities to get us there. Is it hard? Not exactly... but I want to teach you as many tricks as possible so that you have the most success on your travels.

Let's start simple. Follow Charlie and I as we head off for a dispersed campsite, and we'll demonstrate how it's usually done.

A Drive into the Woods

Here's the most common scenario:

We're headed down the highway. It's beginning to get late in the afternoon, and the route seems to be gaining elevation as it crosses into National Forest territory. Glancing at the map, I can see that beyond the National Forest lies a long stretch of towns and farmland. Probably should take advantage of the public acreage while it's close at hand.

We get off the highway at a random exit where roads branch off into the National Forest. One road slants uphill more than the others, so we take it and keep on driving. We pass several spur roads that are identified with white numbers on brown fiberglass markers. Eventually, we choose one of these roads that seems within Charlie's capabilities and follow it until we reach a level spot near where it dead-ends. The area has obviously been logged in the last ten years, exposing a tremendous view of some surrounding peaks. We park right in the middle of the road, as the chances of encountering another vehicle up here seem astronomically low. I also pitch my tent on the level roadbed, and I set my camp chair facing the vista so that I can take in the scenery at my leisure while making an evening meal.

That's all it takes.

More often than not, you'll find a previously-used site with a fire ring, some fallen logs for seating and an adjacent area of flattened ground where you can park or pitch a tent without destroying vegetation. Most National Forests are absolutely riddled with places like this.

Don't *ever* drive onto a virgin meadow or set up camp in any kind of unused, sensitive area. Chances are you won't get busted, but it's the worst kind of nature karma you can acquire. The ghost of John Muir will haunt your dreams, and marmots will chew your radiator hose. Likewise, if there isn't a fire ring already built, you don't *really* need to build one, do you?

National Forests tend to be crisscrossed with old logging roads, and I like to follow them to the tops of ridges so I can camp where the best long-distance views can be found. Just beware of lightning storms! Alternatively, you can head downhill and find shady pullouts next to streams where it's easier to wash up at the end of a dusty day.

Yes, finding a dispersed campsite can be an adventure in itself. You need to be willing to leave things to chance and have fun with the unexpected. With a little practice, even if you misjudge the time and end up searching in the dark, you can have great success. And when you crawl out of your tent in the morning, your surroundings can be yet another surprise.

If you feel you need a little extra help finding your first renegade campsites after reading this book, I put together a short guide listing ten of the best options for your first forays into cross-country car camping, all chosen for their accessibility, natural beauty and capacity to handle the extra attention. It's called *Ten Renegade Camping Destinations in the Western States: Free*

Public Camping Areas Big Enough to Fit You and a Dozen of Your Closest Friends. You can get it free at *www.offthemapbooks.com/freebook.*

Gathering Information

If you're not too confident about the terrain ahead, visit National Forest ranger stations and BLM visitor centers to get information about road conditions and to ask advice about places to do dispersed camping. National Park visitor centers can advise you on the fastest way to find dispersed camping *outside* of their particular park. They're used to those questions because park campgrounds can fill up quickly in summertime.

BLM Camping

Signs for BLM roads have their own unique triangular look to them, and the roads themselves are usually unpaved. Streamside or mountaintop campsites can be harder to come by because BLM lands tend to be drier and flatter. The routes through these landscapes were built by extractive industries, more than likely, and lead to mines and quarries... sometimes ghost towns. Camping in these forgotten corners of our country can be a great way to get acquainted with the bust and boom cycles of the American West.

Reservoirs

When looking for a free place to car-camp for the night, definitely check these places out. Oftentimes as a condition of flooding a vast landscape, the public entity (federal, state, county or city) responsible is required to provide public access and amenities, including boat docks and campgrounds. When close to large population centers, the campgrounds aren't free... but away from cities, they frequently are, with shelters, vault toilets and fire rings often included in the package.

If no campgrounds exist, most rural reservoirs have dirt roads that run parallel to their shorelines, and one may usually engage in dispersed camping along the banks or bluffs. On a hot day, there's nothing like a refreshing swim before setting up camp for the night. And stars or moonlight reflected upon the water's surface will enrich any camping experience.

Private Timberlands

Though not public, some stretches of private timberlands allow dispersed camping and other forms of recreation within their boundaries. Check the signs before you enter. The locations of these forests are hard to predict because they aren't labeled on common maps.

While searching for a campsite, you will drive past stands where the trees are all of equal ages, giving an industrial feeling to the landscape. Be careful of blind corners during your search, because logging trucks are notoriously reckless and have the right-of-way every time.

I've never been able to find long-distance views in private timberlands... perhaps because, unlike in National Forests, new trees are planted very soon after their predecessors are cut down. Cleared meadows don't stay cleared for very long.

Charlie and I tend to avoid camping in these areas unless we have no other options. Though I've never been disturbed, it's still strangely difficult to trust that we will be left alone.

Abandoned Bridges and Roads

Decommissioned bridges can make excellent renegade campsites. I've used them on multiple occasions when the likelihood of my being disturbed seemed minimal. They provide a nice flat surface for tents. The downside is that you can't drive tent stakes into the asphalt or concrete, so staking out a tent's rainfly is impossible.

One solution on rainy days is to tie dead branches to the rainfly guylines and throw the branches off opposite sides of the bridge. Their weight will keep the guylines taut so the rainfly doesn't flap in the wind or blow away.

Decommissioned sections of roads can serve as campsites, too. Look for mountain roads that disappear into tunnels, or places where the road passes through a gap in a ridgeline that was obviously cleared with dynamite. Oftentimes you can see where the original road once traveled a longer distance around the ridgeline. Though overgrown with weeds, these abandoned cliffside roads can serve as emergency campsites. But you might want to leave your vehicle at the barrier gate and hike down the road a ways before you pitch a tent. That will give you some privacy so that you don't have to listen to highway traffic all night.

Town Parks

Another overlooked free camping option is town or city parks. Several towns in the west with populations under 2,000 open up portions of their parks to RVs and tent campers. For free! Don't expect this windfall everywhere, and know that it's not likely to be advertised apart from signage at the park itself. You can check with the local chamber of commerce or visitor center to see if it's possible.

In town parks, you'll find a nice, mowed, grassy place for a tent, and a frequently-clean bathroom with flush toilets. Nearby is likely to be a pavilion with electricity for charging your gear. The downside to these parks is that they have the potential to be noisy. And some parks are directly adjacent to the main thoroughfare through town.

These campsites can be extremely useful in the Great Plains states where public land is scarce, and it's a great way to experience small-town life. Here's an amusing excerpt from my journal entry of September 2, 2005, where I meet the mayor of Buffalo, North Dakota:

"It would have been fun to stop in Fargo, North Dakota and listen to the accents, but I drove on to the city of Cassleton where my cheap camping book told me of free camping at the city park. Unfortunately, the signage there said otherwise. However, not far from Cassleton was the town of Buffalo, population 250, whose city park was also listed as a place to camp. It was a quaint town with dirt streets and a well-kept appearance. I eyeballed the park and was skeptical that camping would be allowed there. So I visited the town's only restaurant, Clem & Hazel's Corner Café. I bought a cheeseburger and asked the waitress about the park. She didn't think camping there would be a problem.

I didn't see anyone leave the building during my meal, but ten minutes later the mayor walked in, looked at me, and said I could camp in the park. Word travels impossibly fast around here! He sat down with some grandmothers, and from the conversation it sounded like the town's biggest problem amounted to backyard thistles and a rogue dachshund that was scratching up people's front doors. I ate dessert, signed the guestbook, and Hazel gave me an official café frisbee! The mayor, Bill, shared some advice about Theodore Roosevelt National Park before I left to go back to the baseball park. Late tonight, after brushing my teeth, I was heading back to my tent when I looked to the north and noticed the Northern Lights! It wasn't a great display, but it was the real thing – not so much curtains of pale green light, but rather like the flashlights of giants being waved in slow-motion."

Power Lines and Cell Towers

In a pinch, these high-voltage environments can come to the rescue of the renegade camper, especially in states where public land is hard to come by. They come in two varieties.

Commonly, where power lines pass through forests, the land on either side is kept clear of trees in order to reduce power outages during storms. If you can gain access to these ribbons of open land, there are jeep roads that run between the transmission towers to allow for maintenance. You will have to ignore the subtle crackling of electricity flowing through the wires overhead should you choose to camp along the ribbons. I personally doubt that 12 hours of exposure to the electro-magnetic fields will harm your body's chemistry, but I still wouldn't camp beneath power lines for more than one night in a row. It just feels unnatural.

Cell towers are built on leased property atop the high points of hills and mountains. Typically these places are public land, so don't feel bad about using access roads or camping in the cleared spaces surrounding the towers. Just try not to attract attention. Don't build campfires, don't play loud music, and don't climb the chain-link fences protecting the cell tower infrastructure. The doors to all buildings are locked anyway. Not that I would know that...

Water Tanks and Towers

Along the ridgelines above cities, you may find a series of concrete water tanks shaped like flat, circular disks. The upper surface is slightly curved so that rainwater collects and trickles down into a small reservoir – possibly to fight fires or for an obsolete purpose.

These are incredibly scenic but slightly risky places to camp. The smooth upper surface is perfect for sleeping under the stars with friends, and sunrise/sunset views can be unforgettable. But water tanks are frequent party spots for teenagers, so they can attract police attention. The police are probably not going to care one way or another about renegade campers, but your solitude is certainly not guaranteed. I recommend avoiding these sites on Friday and Saturday nights, just to be safe.

The same caution goes for the hilltops that hold the larger-sized water towers and tanks containing the municipal water supply. Like cell phone towers, they can provide isolated spaces to camp for a night, with commanding views, but you don't want to attract unnecessary attention while you're there. Park your vehicle behind the water tank where it can't be seen from town and try not to create bright lights at nighttime. Consider alternative sites on weekends or holidays, or you might find your campsite taken over by a rave or a kegger... though that might not be a bad thing, depending on your social inclinations.

Hot Springs

Ah, the pinnacle of the renegade camping experience. Yes, there are places where you can soak in stone tubs of luxurious steaming water, watching the stars overhead through the silhouettes of trees, and once every muscle is sufficiently relaxed, you can crawl into your tent and slip effortlessly into dreams. The best part is that you can do this for free, if you know where to look.

Natural hot springs come in two types: developed and primitive. Developed springs are almost always on private land and will cost a fee for their use. Primitive hot springs, on the other hand, are free, open to the public, and can be out in the middle of nowhere. You may have to drive an hour down rutted dirt roads to reach one. Or hike for ten miles. Or they might be found along a river right next to a major highway. There may be a pit toilet or a changing room nearby, or the site might be primitive in every sense of the word. If there are benches, or if the tubs are lined with cement and fancy tilework, the features were probably built by volunteers.

To find primitive hot springs, plenty of books will point you in the right direction. I use Hot Springs & Hot Pools of the Northwest and Southwest – two books by Marjorie Gersh-Young. In the entries on primitive springs, they also mention whether dispersed camping is available nearby. NOAA's interactive hot springs map at *maps.ngdc.noaa.gov/viewers/hot_springs* is another good resource.

When you're too poor to pay for youth hostels or buy a drink at a local bar, hot springs can be a great way to socialize and meet fellow travelers. Some springs have a self-appointed "caretaker" who camps nearby and who drains and scours the tubs regularly so that algae and sediment don't build up. Be sure to thank him for his efforts, even if he threatens to talk your ears off.

Primitive hot springs are clothing-optional, with people most likely to soak naked in the evening rather than the daytime. Go with whatever you're comfortable with. And enjoy yourself... you've earned it.

THREE

YOUR RENEGADE CAMPSITE

Okay, so now that you've found a suitable place to park the car... how do you make it the best campsite possible? There's no toilet. No picnic table. No electricity. No lights. Are you expected to sleep in a ditch? How do you get comfortable in such primitive conditions?

First of all, *relax*. Charlie and I have lots of tricks we can teach you from our twenty summers of cross-country travel. We won't leave you stranded. We've got suggestions for gear and for campsite routines that will make you feel comfortable in no time.

Vehicles

If you're looking for advice on how to convert a van or truck into living quarters, there are plenty of great guides - online and in print - that will get you pointed in the right direction. Once you have your infrastructure in place, it can be a great way to save money on the road, and it can give you more options when you're stuck in a downpour or lost in a city. Such conversions are beyond my expertise; I would suggest reading How to Live in a Car, Van or RV: And Get Out of Debt, Travel, and Find True Freedom, by Bob Wells.

On my first adult cross-country journey, my partner and I slept in the back of Charlie almost every night when we renegade-camped, rather than pitch a tent. This decision required a laborious ritual of emptying out the sleeping area and stacking all our equipment on the front seats. Next trip, I learned my lesson. I started setting up the tent every night, and I continue that practice to this day. More on that later.

If you have a choice of vehicles, keep in mind; the higher the clearance, the more options you will have when choosing a campsite. Some of the best sites require some creative maneuvering when the boulders sticking out of the road threaten to gouge your oil pan. Take care not to exceed your off-roading skill level or your vehicle's capabilities.

Tents

This may be your home for months at a time. Choose wisely.

I recommend two tents. For backpacking, have a tent on hand that is lightweight and no bigger than what you need. For car camping, buy a tent that is big, sturdy, and as heavy as it needs to be. These heavier tents can be quite inexpensive – as cheap as $25 at a sporting goods store. Don't buy a palace-sized tent unless you plan to stay in one location for multiple days. You want a tent you can pitch in five minutes.

The system of tent poles is the biggest factor in the set-up time required. Modern backpacking tents have complex, spiderlike networks of interconnected poles that minimize weight and maximize strength but are time-consuming to assemble and take apart. The best car camping tents, I have found, use a simple X-shaped pole system. Grab the poles by the central hub, shake them out so the four arms dangle and snap lengthwise on their own, then plug the arms into the hub. Easy.

I would only add the rainfly when rain or dust storms threaten, to keep out heavy dewfall near streams, to conserve heat, to minimize moonlight, or for privacy.

Now, are you ready for the best secret of all?

A full-sized inflatable mattress. Eight inches thick. About twenty bucks.

If you have one of these, you no longer have to search your campsite for the flattest possible area. A thick mattress underneath your tent will smooth out rocks and bumps, and it feels much more comfortable than only having a sleeping pad between you and the ground. Get a pump that plugs into the 12-volt outlet of your vehicle. I usually throw the mattress on the top of my jeep and inflate it there.

So here's my system. I lay down the tent's footprint (some people use a tarp) first, to keep the mattress clean and puncture-free. Then I inflate and lay the mattress on the footprint. The tent goes on top of that. If needed, the rainfly follows, and I personally use a tent whose rainfly covers the mattress. A full-sized mattress is usually adequate for two people; the corners of a queen-sized mattress may extend too far past the rainfly and get wet during a storm. Of course, if you use a tent big enough to stand in, the mattress may easily fit inside, which simplifies matters.

I love this system. On a rainy night, stretching out on a thick mattress is exquisitely cozy. But there is one potential downside. On cold nights, the outside air can cool the air within the mattress faster than your body heat can warm it. Too much volume in an eight-inch thick mattress. To prevent waking up shivering at 3 o'clock in the morning, put a sleeping bag or a thin sleeping pad beneath you when you sleep. Inflatable backpacking pads are thin enough that your body heat can keep them warm through the night. Foam pads can work even better.

Vehicle Positioning

Some renegade campsites, especially in the desert, can have significant wind exposure. Windstorms can begin in the evening and last all night. In these situations, I highly recommend parking perpendicular to the prevailing winds and using your vehicle as a windblock. Usually, this means pitching your tent on the east side of your vehicle and tying one of the rainfly guylines to the tires or undercarriage.

More often, you will find yourself needing to block the morning sunlight instead of the wind, particularly in those treeless desert expanses during the summer season. Pay attention to where the sun is setting, orient your car north-to-south and pitch your tent on the west side of the vehicle. The sun will rise in the east, and you will have gained a precious few hours of shade before the sun rises high enough to bake your tent and make further sleep impossible.

Bedding

Don't sleep in your sleeping bag every night. They don't breathe well, and they can get really dirty over time. Instead, throw bedsheets and a comforter into the tent, along with a full-sized pillow. Put the sleeping bag on top of your bedding or underneath you if you're expecting a cold night.

Is it a hassle to transfer the bedding from your tent to the vehicle every morning? Then just leave the pillows, sleeping bag and blanket inside the tent. Take out the poles, grab the tent by the corners and toss the whole lot into the back of your vehicle. Throw your camp chair or the rolled-up mattress on top to weigh the tent down so you can still see out the rear window. With this method, setting up your bedding each evening is also a much faster process, plus your tent won't blow away while you're trying to insert the tent poles.

Empty the tent completely once a week, at least, just so you can shake out any hair, food particles or debris that may accumulate.

Water Sources

Having a five or six-gallon water container is key to cross-country travel. Free campgrounds are almost exclusively without water infrastructure, and dispersed campsites don't always come with clean streams nearby. To fill your container for free, you can use the spigots on the sides of visitor center buildings or the outdoor faucets at highway rest areas. Many states require their gas stations to provide free outdoor faucets. It's also acceptable to drive into non-free federal campgrounds and fill a container or two; no one ever minds as long as you obey the campground speed limit.

When necessary, you can filter or boil water from streams. To conserve water supplies, I use stream water for soups or pasta since it has to be boiled anyway.

Showering

> **SHOWER INSTRUCTIONS**
> 1. TURN SHOWER VALVE OFF
> 2. INSERT TOKEN
> 3. DEPRESS TOKEN SLIDE
> 4. WATER FLOW IS APPROX. 8.5 MINUTES
> 5. TURN SHOWER VALVE OFF

Sometimes there's just no substitute for a good shower. At some private campgrounds, youth hostels, bunkhouses, YMCAs or fitness centers you can pay a flat fee and get a long, hot shower before continuing on to a dispersed campsite for the night. Other public and private campgrounds have coin-operated showers where, if you're an efficient scrubber, a good rinse can be had for even less money.

But if you just need to wash the day's sweat off your body, score yourself a renegade streamside campsite. Immerse yourself in the water if possible, or just stand in the current and use a wet washcloth to scrub yourself down. No soap necessary. If you can't find a water source, use your five-gallon water container and washcloth. Scrub yourself down head to toe, rinsing and wringing out the washcloth periodically. This can be a chilly practice on cold evenings, but good hygiene is critical to sustaining one's physical and emotional well-being on extended cross-country adventures.

Cold water not your thing? Get a solar shower for $10-$20. It's a black PVC bag that you fill with water from a stream or spigot and lay out on a hot surface like the hood of a car until it warms sufficiently. Hang the bag from a tree branch, turn the attached nozzle, and you've got yourself a warm shower! On long driving days, I suggest placing a half-filled bag on the sill above your dashboard so that the sun can warm the bag through the windshield.

A worthy upgrade is the pressure shower. These collapsible units, which range from $35-$100, sit on the ground and hold about three gallons of water. The foot pump adds pressure to the system, and then you can use the long hose and spray nozzle to douse and rinse yourself efficiently. They can also be left in the sun to heat up, and they're equally useful for rinsing off dishes and camping gear. Perhaps they're a bit much for a solo traveler who camps in a new location each night, but for multi-day stays or group settings, a pressure shower can be a valuable addition to your renegade camping arsenal.

Lighting

Forget the flashlight. Nothing beats a good headlamp for enabling you to keep your hands free while cooking or setting up your tent in the dark.

No, wait... there is one thing. Luci makes a $15 inflatable solar lantern that is extraordinarily useful and lightweight enough to take backpacking. Charge it up by placing it atop your dashboard or clipping it to your backpack. You can get ten hours of light before it needs to be charged up again. I use the lantern inflated on a picnic table to light up the space, and when it's deflated, I wedge the little disc into an upper pocket of my tent to provide ambient light while I'm arranging the bedding. Brought closer, the light is more than sufficient to read by before I go to sleep.

I don't normally do product endorsement, but these little beauties are cheap enough that it won't set you back much to follow my advice. Buy one. *And* a headlamp.

Cooking

If cooking is a quintessential part of your camping experience, sure... get a two-burner propane stove. For two or more people traveling together, a large stove system might benefit group morale and logistics.

But if you're solo and no culinary expert, make it simple. I use an MSR Whisperlite stove because they last for years and years, plus I can take mine backpacking when I need to. They run efficiently and use white gas for fuel. If I'm car camping for a string of nights, I don't bother breaking the unit down. I wrap a plastic grocery bag around the stove to keep the soot contained, then I toss it into the jeep.

Eating primarily at your campsite, as opposed to dining out, is crucial to keeping expenses down while on the road. Save your money, and splurge on restaurants when you really need to, like on rainy days.

Shelter

But if you absolutely must cook on a rainy day, it helps to have a tarp at hand. Tie 6-10 feet of string to each corner, and tie a loop at the end of each string. Attach a heavy object like a metal carabiner to one of the loops, and throw the carabiner over a tree branch. The weight of the carabiner will help pull the string down to where you can reach it. Retrieve the carabiner, tie the string to a lower branch, and repeat with the other three strings until your tarp is held aloft between four trees. Make sure the tarp is taut and tilted so water spills off and does not accumulate. Now you can light your stove and prepare an evening meal without rainwater dripping down your neck. When you pack up the tarp, leave the strings attached for the sake of efficiency.

If you're camping at one site for several days, you may want to be proactive and set up a tarp shelter just in case, even if rain isn't in the forecast.

Washing the Dishes

Want to make it simple? Don't use soap. If you're camping in a large group at campgrounds, sure.... use a system with multiple tubs of water. You can even use Earth-friendly, biodegradable liquid soap in the process. But when *I* camp solo or camp with a partner, I don't bother. I use napkins.

My best friend in the camping kitchen is the unbleached napkin. You can buy them in household-use packages, but I prefer the cheap, 500-pack bundles made for the food industry from recycled materials. They have no bad toxins or chemicals, so if loose pieces go astray in your campsite, they will decompose quickly and blend in with the environment while they do.

Napkins are great for cleaning up oily residues on pans, pots and silverware, as long as you dispose of the napkins with your trash. Sometimes no further scrubbing is necessary. Bacteria love damp environments, like water coolers and Tupperware; minuscule dry food particles on pots and pans are not a good medium for bacterial growth. Still, if a pot has a dried film on it, I'll usually follow up with a wet napkin scrub and one last napkin for drying. I don't use sponges because they get oily and need rinsing with soap eventually.

Some pots get fairly clean just by adding water and swishing it around, in addition to using a napkin to scrub off the residue. But whether you get your water from a container or from a stream, make sure you splash the dirty water on land, away from water sources and your campsite. In most dispersed camping areas, food particles are infrequently added to the environment, so the local wildlife don't have the opportunity to become habituated to food scraps and turn into scavengers. Just think twice before you throw half a plate of spaghetti into the forest, or even a single piece of pasta. Scrape the big pieces into your trash before doing your dishes. Wild animals don't stay wild if careless campers are abundant.

Here's an important disclaimer. I seldom cook meat while renegade camping, probably because I don't like the hassle and expense of buying ice for my cooler. If you're cooking eggs or meat, the protocol changes. To keep yourself from getting foodborne illnesses, you'd probably better use soap when washing up. At the very least, heat your pots or pans to a high temperature on your stove for a few minutes before adding food to them the next time you cook. This will kill off any bacteria that may have grown in the interim.

Seating

Fold-up camping chairs take up space, but they're worth it. They can be as cheap as $10, so bring one for each member of your party. They're much more adjustable than a rock when you need to scoot away from the campfire because of heat or smoke.

A second chair type, quite useful in camping, is the legless "stadium seat", used often in the bleachers at sports events. This chair consists of two padded squares - one to sit on and one to lean back against. Your body weight and two pieces of webbing provide the tension to keep it in a chair-like shape. These seats take up little space in your vehicle, but they are nice for picnic tables and excellent for tents. I use Charlie's 12-volt adapter to charge my laptop while driving, and then I can sit comfortably in my stadium-style chair in my tent at night and watch a movie before bed.

Toilet Training

If your significant other is not comfortable squatting in the woods, this aspect of dispersed camping can be a deal-breaker. Explaining the options to them requires some... finesse.

The traditional method is to dig a hole with a trowel six inches deep. Next, you do your business. Your business goes in the hole. The toilet paper goes in the hole. You cover the hole. Then you wash your hands or use hand sanitizer. No big deal.

However, I've seen too much toilet paper strewn about on public lands to know that curious animals will dig up these holes if they're not deep enough. I don't like to give them the option. I burn my toilet paper.

Yep. I make a pile on a rock, a bare patch of earth scraped free of leaves, or on the ruts of whatever dirt road I'm camped near. I light the stack on fire and use a stick to stir the papers so that all the fibers get consumed. If there are embers left, I pour a little water on top to be on the safe side. Done! No chance of an unsightly mess should skunks come wandering by.

Now, lest you think I've left several forest fires in my wake, there are caveats to this method. If it's windy, a flaming piece of toilet paper can travel pretty far. Bury it instead. If the forest around you is a drought-ravaged tinderbox waiting for a single spark to set it off, forget it. Far more often than not, however, you will be able to safely dispose of your t.p. in this manner.

And for people with predictable bowel movements, there is always this option: wake up, pack up the tent, then drive to a highway rest area, gas station or fee campground and use a proper toilet.

Flat Tires, Dead Batteries

I have been amazed by the kindness of strangers... people who appear out of nowhere and are willing to patch your tires or tow your vehicle out of a mud pit. Nevertheless, the true renegade camper learns over time to be self-reliant so that they, too, have the capacity to help those less fortunate. This means learning how to change a tire and jump-start a car.

At the bare minimum, you should always travel with a spare tire, a jack, and jumper cables. You should know how to jack up your vehicle and replace the tire; practice in your driveway if you need to. Of course, I have gotten two flat tires at the same time before. In that instance, I was lucky to find help in the middle of nowhere, but now I carry two additional bits of renegade survival gear: a tire repair kit and an air compressor that plugs into a 12-volt outlet.

To use a tire repair kit, you have to find the hole in the tire first. Sometimes the hole isn't obvious; you may have to jack up the tire, inflate it with an air compressor, and pour water on the tire tread to make it easier to hear the air escaping. Once the hole is located, use a metal reamer from the kit to abrade the hole, then add glue to a rubber tire plug and jam it in the hole. After you've repaired a tire once this way, it gets pretty easy, and the tire probably won't ever need to be taken to a shop and patched.

A simpler process for flat repair is to use a tire puncture sealant like "Fix-A-Flat", which comes in aerosol cans that you attach right to the tire valve stem. The contents are released into the tire, where they coat the surfaces and prevent air from escaping. This, however, is a temporary fix. You will still have to take the tire to a shop, where the mechanics will clean off the chemicals and apply an actual patch.

Dead batteries are another annoyingly familiar problem for the renegade traveler, but having a real-time indicator of your battery's strength will help you avoid surprises. You can pick up a car battery voltage monitor that plugs into your 12-volt outlet for about $7. The $12 model comes with USB charging ports and features a digital display of your battery's voltage so you can stop charging your appliances before the car battery drains too far.

Jumper cables are essential for restarting a dead battery, but they require a second vehicle to come to your assistance. If you wish to bolster your independence, consider purchasing a portable power pack. These units contain a battery that can be charged via any household outlet and used to jump-start a vehicle, charge a phone, or run a number of appliances. Some power packs include an air compressor, too. The devices may be a worthwhile investment, especially if you like to be able to car camp in one location for a few days without having to leave to charge your electronics.

If your car has a manual transmission, you should also know the trick to "push-starting" a vehicle with a dead battery. Put the car in second gear, depress the clutch, turn the ignition switch to the "on" position, and get some bystanders to push the vehicle until it reaches 5-10 miles per hour. Next, you "pop the clutch" by taking your foot off the clutch pedal – this will make the engine rotate and fire. The engine may want to immediately stall again, so quickly give the car some gas and/or depress the clutch once more. Don't forget to let the engine run for a significant time afterward and let the battery recharge, or you'll be back in the same predicament the next time you try to start your car.

If you know your vehicle has chronic battery issues, try to park on a road facing downhill when you find a campsite for the night. Even if you're all by yourself, you can execute the same push-starting trick by releasing the brakes and rolling forward until your vehicle reaches 5-10 miles per hour. Pointing downhill when parking is a good habit to get into. Think of it as insurance for the renegade camper; sooner or later, you'll be glad you prepared for the possibility of a dead battery.

While we're talking worst-case scenarios, you should *also* prepare for the possibility of getting locked out of your vehicle, especially because it's bound to happen when you're miles away from cell reception. I had to break Charlie's window once to retrieve a spare key after losing my keychain in the San Rafael Wilderness. Took him a long time to forgive me.

Now I have a magnetic key case attached to the underside of the jeep, which has served me well in several urban situations when I locked my keys inside the vehicle. Find a horizontal section of your undercarriage and wipe it clean before attaching a case with a spare key – that way the magnet will make full contact with the metal. Use an upper surface if possible so gravity works in your favor. Charlie and I have traveled countless teeth-rattling roads without our key case shaking loose, so I can vouch for the strength of the magnets in those little units. Just don't forget where you attached the case, or you'll get your hands and knees rather dirty while searching for it.

The Secret to Renegade Camping Peace-of-Mind

Sometimes, you're just not quite sure *where* you are. Perhaps you're uncertain if camping is allowed at your location, and maybe the signs and boundary markers around you are all ambiguous. Renegade campers can find themselves in this situation *a lot*. It's no fun if you're feeling anxious, wondering if the authorities are going to drive by and roust you, or whether some absentee landowner is going to make a surprise appearance. But there's one simple thing you can do to give yourself peace of mind... *and* it's good for the planet: pick up a bag of trash.

Yep. Just use a thin plastic grocery bag or a used Ziploc and scour your campsite for beer cans, shotgun cartridges, cigarette butts... all the stuff you might expect to find in these neglected regions. Then if some unexpected land manager drives into your campsite, you can introduce yourself, apologize for not knowing the land was private, show them the trash you've collected and ask if it's okay to stay until morning. You can promise that you'll leave the land looking better than the condition in which you found it. A goodwill gesture like that should do wonders to win over the locals.

Now, I'd like to point out that I have yet to be challenged or disturbed in any of the "questionably-legal" campsites that I've used over the years. It's easy to get worked up over the possibility of an irate landowner showing up with a shotgun, especially when you're camping solo. But it's just not likely to ever happen. I've never had to use a bag of trash as a peace token, and yet I still do it, just because it dispels any concerns about how I might be treated, and it helps me settle into my campsite.

So bag that litter. At the least, you'll improve the aesthetics of your temporary home and enrich the natural experience for future travelers.

Leave No Trace

The "Leave No Trace" principles are guidelines that promote conservation in the outdoors. If you're a renegade camper, listen closely; most of these apply to you as well. We don't want to be known for mucking up the natural environment, nor do we want additional regulations regarding the use of dispersed camping on public lands because of a few bad apples.

First and foremost, choose well-used campsites. If you're parking on grass, you're probably doing it wrong. If you have to move rocks to stabilize your tent or for any other reason, move them back before you leave the site. Likewise, if you need to remove a bunch of pinecones and twigs in order to pitch your tent, scatter some afterward to restore the natural look of the area.

Don't dig trenches around your tent. Don't nail anything into trees; tie ropes around limbs instead if you need to hang something. And when going to a stream to collect water, be careful not to step on sensitive vegetation.

Don't try to ride the animals. Don't mess with their homes. Don't feed them, accidentally or otherwise. If you need to leave camp for a short while, make sure all food is safely stored in your vehicle.

If there's not a fire ring in your campsite already, skip having a fire unless your dinner absolutely depends on it. Build campfires responsibly; don't make a bonfire, and never light fires in windy conditions. Only use downed branches for firewood. If there is time and the air is calm, allow wood and coals to burn down to ash, then pour water on top to make sure the coals are out completely.

Be considerate of other visitors to public lands. Keep the volume of your speakers at a reasonable level, and don't use them at all if anyone is camping nearby. Not everybody likes to hear the Allman Brothers at midnight or Tom Jones at 8 o'clock in the morning.

Bury human waste at least six inches below the surface and at least 200 feet away from streams or lakes. If you have to use soap for your hands or dishes, use small amounts of biodegradable soap and use it well away from water sources.

Of course, pack out your trash and don't burn anything plastic in your campfire. Don't leave food scraps in the kitchen area when you go to sleep at night. And do one last sweep for trash before you depart the next morning. It's nice to be able to drive away with a clear conscience, knowing you've left the place in better condition than that in which you found it. Plus, when you're essentially relying on luck every night to find a campsite, it helps to accrue some good renegade camping karma.

FOUR

ROAD RESOURCES

Now that we've walked you through the process of finding dispersed campsites on public land, we're going use our remaining time to discuss the resources available to the thrifty traveler while *away* from the campsite. When budgets are tight, these cost-saving measures can help free up funds for what you really want, like a ticket to Burning Man.

But first, a reminder about the emotional landscape that lies ahead.

The Loneliness Factor

The sad truth about traveling cheaply is that it can be an isolated endeavor. Dispersed camping in and of itself provides no opportunity for human interaction outside your group. To keep costs down, you'll need to cook on a camp stove rather than eat at restaurants and cafés. You'll probably need to go sparingly on the alcohol and purchase your own beer and spirits rather than pay barroom prices, sad as that sounds (plus, the difficulty of searching for dispersed campsites in the dark makes evening barroom hangouts impractical anyways). Unfortunately, the most common forms of social entertainment available to a stranger in an unfamiliar town require money.

"Don't you get lonely?" is a question I frequently hear on the road, since I tend to hike, camp and drive solo in summertime. "Not really," I usually respond... but I know I am an anomaly. I've always had an extensive capacity for solo time, and I love the solitude that dispersed camping provides. Still, I can recommend some inexpensive social outlets that will keep your conversational skills from atrophying.

When passing through mid-sized towns, I keep an ear out for open mic nights at coffeehouses and bars. Unlike the typical barroom situation, it is fairly easy to meet locals at these events and strike up a conversation. The people that come to listen or to entertain are naturally gregarious. Come early to put your name on a list, and the host will call you up to the small stage for your 5 to 15 minutes of fame. It's a great place to share a story, a song on the ukulele, or the poem you just wrote that morning back at your campsite. Audiences are very forgiving, and as long as you don't take yourself too seriously, they'll even applaud your failures.

With a subtle hint, you might even land a place to stay for the night. But the entertainment alone usually makes it worth having to search for a campsite in the dark afterward. Don't forget to support the establishment by buying at least one drink. And sign up early, so you don't end up having to wait until past midnight to perform.

My other recommendation... is couchsurfing.

Couchsurfing

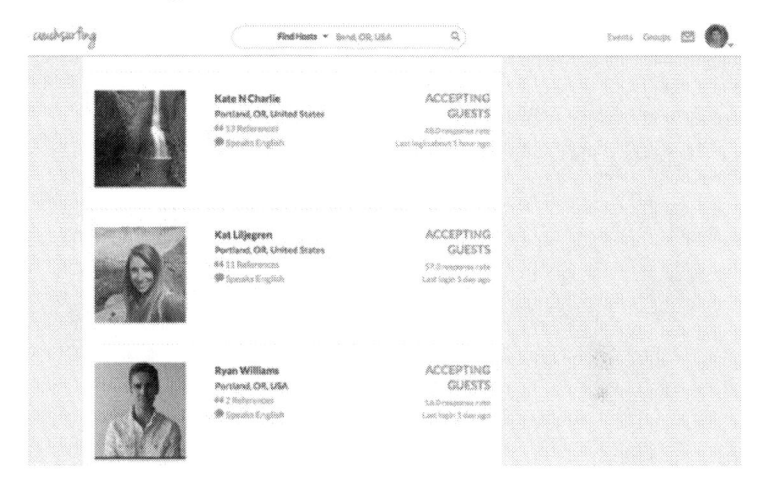

If you need a place to stay while traveling, you can always couchsurf at the homes of your personal friends, sure. Visitation might even be the express purpose for your trip. But what if you're in a strange town or city, and friendless?

Welcome to *couchsurfing.com*. The official Couchsurfing organization is a network of millions of people all around the world who are willing to let you crash on their couch or in a guest bedroom for free. No exchange of money allowed. Be prepared to share stories, though; the people signed on to the network are usually seasoned travelers or young explorers who hope to have their hospitality reciprocated at a later date. After a stay, both the host and the guest rate their experience as positive or negative on the website and give a review; this provides a level of accountability similar to eBay and other online companies.

How it works is that you type your destination city into the website. A list of potential hosts appears, ranked by how responsive each host is to couchsurfing requests. Click on a few names, read through their bio and reviews, and make a note of their location within the city. Most hosts like to hear that they and their potential guests have some shared interest in common. Once you find a suitable match, use the website to send a couch-surfing request, telling the host a little about yourself, when you would expect to arrive, and how many days you'd like to stay. I almost always crash for only one night, although some hosts appreciate multi-day stopovers and love to give tours through their hometown. Some even like to provide dinner, but I never count on this happening. A small gift of wine or a suitable beverage would be appropriate to bring just in case a meal is offered.

In a matter of hours or days, you will usually get a response from the website. If your preferred host is unable to accommodate you, try the next person on your list. In the user profiles, you will see that some people have no couch available but are still willing to meet up for coffee or give afternoon tours. These folks can also be valuable; sometimes I like to chat with couchsurfers just so I can glean information about cool hikes in an unfamiliar area.

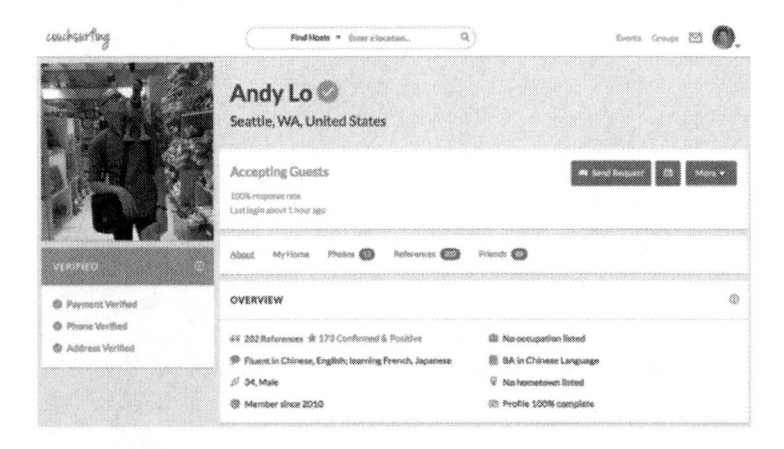

If you're starting out on the website and have no references, potential hosts may have a hard time trusting you enough to bring you inside their homes. You can circumvent this problem by asking friends who use the site to write you a character reference. Or you can ask the same from any other couchsurfer that you meet for coffee. Even better, host some travelers yourself... just get permission from your housemates first!

Couchsurfing is a fantastic way to get a shower, a roof over your head, and have plenty of opportunities for socializing without needing to pay a dime. The downside is that it can diminish flexibility and spontaneity for the renegade traveler. The further in advance you make your couchsurfing request, the more likely it is to be accepted, but the more constrained your traveling schedule becomes. I have couchsurfed my way though Norway and New Zealand, but I had to also hitchhike to save money, and thumbing rides became a little stressful whenever I worried that I might not reach my hosts' hometowns on time. Arriving a day late was never an option... not if I wanted to maintain my online couchsurfing reputation.

Apart from this small issue, I've never had a bad experience with hosting or being hosted. So if you know that a front of bad weather is approaching, or you're passing through a region with minimal public lands, try *www.couchsurfing.com*. It can break up your lonely nights and make cross-country travel much easier. Hosts can become friends... friends who are glad to welcome you back the next time you're drifting through town.

Youth Hostels

After many weeks on the road, the lack of a proper shower can start to undermine your commitment to the camping lifestyle. Your body might ache for a few moments' rest on a sofa or easy chair, or maybe you long to be able to illuminate your surroundings at the flip of a switch. When cravings for the fruits of civilization become overwhelming and there are no couchsurfing options to be found, it may be time to splurge for a night at a youth hostel.

Hostels, which are open to people of all ages, including children, feature modern plumbing and bunkrooms where you can sleep on a moderately-comfortable mattress for a fee of $15 to $30 per night. If you're not inclined to be sociable and if there are more than one of you, it might be more cost-effective to get a cheap motel; the mattresses there are far softer. But for a solo traveler, hostels are a nice treat now and again that won't set your finances back too far.

One way that hostels save you money is that they provide kitchens and cookware for community use. You don't have to eat out at a restaurant if you don't want to. During an all-night downpour, being able to cook and sleep indoors can be an emotional lifesaver. The downside of hostels is that unless you pay extra for a private room, you have to share a bunkroom with several strangers, and the bustling about of people with different late-night and early-morning schedules – not to mention the snoring – can sometimes be intolerable. Having a sleep mask and a pair of earplugs will make you a much happier guest.

In big cities, hostels are very useful because of their proximity to cultural centers. Plus, they are much more affordable than city hotels, even for couples. They are also a great opportunity to meet like-minded travelers, in case you've been feeling deprived of social interaction while car camping solo for extended periods. Hostels have living rooms and other community spaces where you can hang out and engage in conversations with people from all around the world. You might even find people who want to join you on expeditions into the wild.

In the time before Charlie came into my life, I spent several months hitchhiking across the British Isles, sleeping exclusively in hostels. Now I only frequent them every couple years or so. The cost of hostels can add up quickly, especially if you make a habit of using them. To be able to afford my extended travels in the States, I had to find other ways of fulfilling my social needs... but more on that later.

To find out which hostels are out there, there are many websites to choose from. All the hostels affiliated with Hostelling International (over 4,000 in total) must adhere to certain standards regarding amenities and supervision. You must purchase a membership in order to visit HI hostels in many countries, like the United States. Learn more at *www.hihostels.com*. Other hostels not affiliated with HI can be found at *www.hostelworld.com*, and *www.hostelbookers.com*.

AirBnB and Hipcamp

Another option for cheap-but-not-free lodging is AirBnB – a website where people with guest bedrooms or empty houses can rent out those spaces to travelers. There are currently over a million and a half listings on the website in 190 countries. Initially the "Air" in the name stood for "air mattresses", but since those early days, the lodging opportunities have skewed more towards upscale offerings.

A renegade traveler is not going to be able to afford the thousand-dollar-a-day condo listed for Jackson Hole, Wyoming, but you may occasionally want to treat yourself to a comfortable bed in a warm home for $20-$35 a night. The breakfast option – typical of traditional "bed and breakfasts" – is not always available with the low-end listings, but the use of a kitchen may be included.

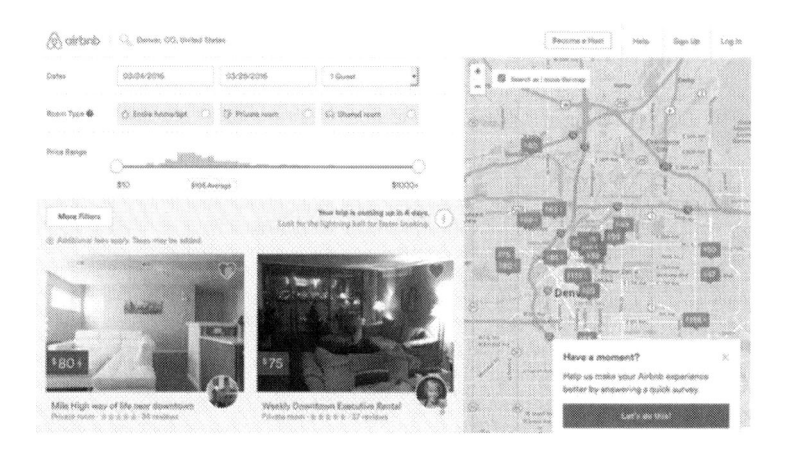

The website works similar to Couchsufing in that every house listing is associated with a user profile, and users can post reviews on their experience as both a guest and a host. After you put in a reservation request, the host has at least 24 hours to accept or decline.

Hosts are able to determine their own cancellation policy, from generous to super strict; make sure you read their terms before making a reservation. As long as you get your money back, I wouldn't feel too bad about having to cancel. It's a business transaction, and fickle customers are part of the cost of doing business. Just be aware that the cancellation will be noted on your user page, which may affect how hosts respond to your requests in the future.

Hipcamp is a remarkably similar enterprise where private property owners can offer camping space on the farms, ranches, vineyards and backyards that they own. Prices are sometimes affordable, but many listings fall into the "glamping" category of overpriced, high-end campsites that feature electricity, camp kitchens, refrigerators, showers and other amenities. Private yurts, guest cabins and trailers are also listed, along with the normal public campgrounds. Check out the website or the Hipcamp app to find some interesting options in urban areas, but be discriminating; if you don't like the idea of paying for tent space, you may wish to save your money for an AirBnB or a motel instead.

Hitchhiking

Wait... if you're renegade car camping, why would you need to know about hitchhiking? For one thing, your car might break down. But the more likely scenario is that you're doing a one-way hike or backpacking trip and you don't want to pay for a shuttle to get back to your vehicle. Or maybe no shuttle service exists.

Hitchhiking is a grand tradition, both in America and across the globe. It's an exercise in faith and patience. You're relying on the goodwill of humanity, and you're bound to meet people from all walks of life, from opera singers to redneck truck drivers. Sometimes you'll even be offered a place to stay the night. In my experience, this can vary from junkyards to abandoned hotels haunted by ghosts. Yes, thumbing rides is safer for men than it is for women. But I've met plenty of female hitchhikers too. You have to consider your exposure to risk, which depends on how isolated your route is.

When you're sticking your thumb out, be sure to take off your sunglasses and headphones, wear a warm smile and, if possible, hold up a sign with the next major city written upon it in black marker. I pack a cardboard cereal box with me when I know I'm going to need a sign at the end of a hike. If you've got a big backpack, make sure it's standing next to you so that drivers can identify you as a backpacker and not a vagabond.

Stand where you can be seen by drivers from as far a distance as possible, and also make sure there is a safe place for vehicles to pull over just past your position. No driver is going to want to risk their life trying to pick up a stranger on a blind corner. If your location is unsuitable, hike down the road until you find a safer and more visible position.

Don't try hitchhiking from the middle of a city or town. If you need to travel to another town or trailhead, hike to the outskirts of the municipality before you put out your thumb. Otherwise, you'll be bothering lots of people who are only traveling short distances within the city.

Lastly, don't waste energy being resentful about the drivers that pass you by. You can't judge them; maybe they're only going a quarter-mile down the road. Maybe they're just not in a mental state to deal with a passenger right now. Maybe it only *looks* like they have room in the car, but every seat is occupied by a vicious chihuahua. Don't stress it. Nobody owes you anything. Just enjoy the fresh air and allow yourself to be pleasantly surprised by the kindness of strangers.

Rideshares

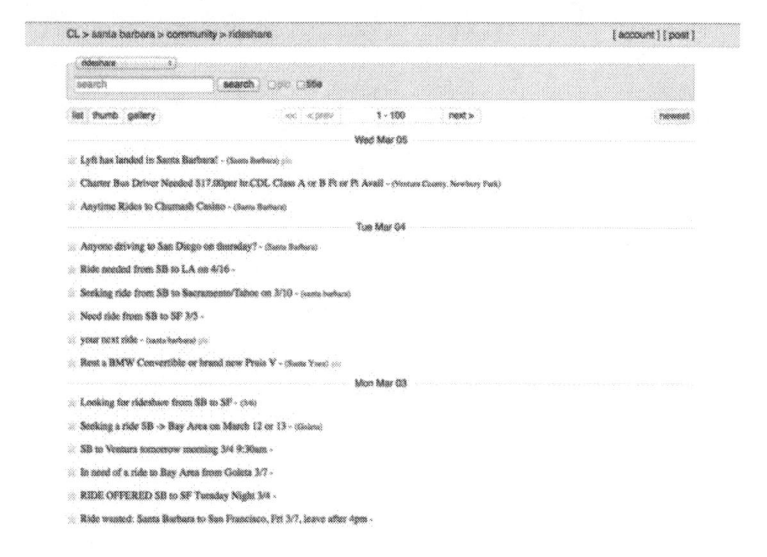

If you're got room in the passenger seat, why not defray the cost of gasoline by taking on a rider? Check out the rideshare section of *www.craigslist.org* and see if anyone needs a lift in the direction you're headed. It might be worth delaying your journey an extra day in order to accommodate a fellow traveler. You can also post your destination ahead of time and solicit passengers that way. You'll undoubtedly end up having some interesting conversations en route.

To prevent misunderstandings, make sure you work out beforehand how much gas money you expect to receive from your passenger.

Backpacking

This is going to sound completely obvious, but incorporating backpacking into your vacation, as opposed to just driving and sightseeing, is something that will bring down your weekly expenses. While you're hiking through the wilderness, you're not eating at restaurants, buying groceries, filling the gas tank or paying for lodging. Your costs will still involve permits (in some areas), stove fuel, food and, of course, all the necessary equipment. Once you acquire the right gear, backpacking becomes one of the cheapest activities you can do while traveling.

If your equipment is over ten years old, I strongly recommend getting rid of it and taking advantage of the technological advances made in materials and designs. Lightweight tents, sleeping pads and backpacks can be a game-changer. I used to hate backpacking before I finally upgraded my equipment and shaved about fifteen pounds off my average load. You'll have to visit high-end outfitters like REI rather than sports outlets in order to find the lightweight stuff.

Consider saving money on meals by purchasing cheap, dehydrated foods like ramen, oatmeal and mac n' cheese. Freeze-dried dinner packages are expensive and can taste like mush if you're not selective. As an alternative, prepare fancy meals beforehand. Plenty of books can be discovered on the subject of outdoor cooking. I would also recommend visiting the websites *www.backpackingchef.com*, *www.adventurediningguide.com*, and *www.food.com/topic/camping* to find delicious camping recipes for your next expedition into the wild.

A willingness to backpack can also save you lots of gas money when you're stuck in a National Park and the campgrounds are full or prohibitively expensive. Instead of driving outside the park to find a dispersed campsite, stop at the Wilderness Office and pick up a backpacking permit. They can be anywhere from free to $10 a day, depending on the park. In some places like Yosemite's Tuolumne Valley, you may have to only hike a mile from the trailhead before you're allowed to pitch a tent. Make dinner before hitting the trail, and you won't have to carry the weight of a stove and cookware. You can wake early and enjoy a leisurely walk back to your vehicle while you build up an appetite for breakfast. Granted, it's a lot of effort just to save a few bucks, but it's nice to have bragging rights that you technically backpacked in some of the most famous places on Earth.

In some popular National Forests, finding roads for dispersed camping can be difficult. If you're stuck for options, you may be able to park at a trailhead, hike for five minutes, then head off-trail to find a private spot for you and your tent. Check if permits are required. If they are, National Forest permits tend to be free.

Free Campgrounds

You don't always have to go renegade if you want to camp for free. To find the assortment of free campgrounds scattered across public lands in the U.S., I recommend Don Wright's book Guide to Free Campgrounds. There really is nothing else like it. Not every listing is up-to-date or completely accurate, but my net experience using the book is very positive. The guide is bloated by the inclusion of all campgrounds $12 and under, so you'll have to ignore most of the listings if you're as stubborn about free camping as I am. Free sites will have level ground, a fire pit, pit toilets, and usually a picnic table. These are your federal tax dollars at work; sign the register if it exists, just so the government knows that their facilities are being used and appreciated.

The most comprehensive online platform that allows people to share information on free and cheap campgrounds is *www.freecampsites.net*. Check it out and add to the listings if you can.

Libraries

Libraries can be an oasis of calm in your road-weary life. You can take a break and charge your electronic devices while you catch up on your social media responsibilities. These days, nearly all libraries provide free wireless access as well as computers that are available to visitors by reservation. If you can use your smartphone as a wireless hotspot for your laptop and tablet, then libraries are somewhat less essential. Yet some library services are hard to replicate elsewhere.

You can borrow a desk computer, research routes on dangerous mountains using *www.peakbagger.com* or *www.summitpost.org*, then print out the essential directions and topo maps for 10 to 20 cents a page. Or you can go to the shelves, grab a guide to local hikes and photocopy the essential pages. To save money, take pictures of the pages using your smartphone or camera so that you can access the images during a hike. Just don't run out of batteries, or you will come to curse your miserly ways. (I suggest switching your phone to airplane mode until you need to send out that all-important mountaintop selfie.)

For a traveling writer like myself, libraries are invaluable. My weekly writing schedule forces me to relax in a comfortable chair by a window at least one day each week, which allows my muscles and joints to recover from overuse. Whenever possible, I arrange my writing days to fall during periods of bad weather so that I don't feel bad about being stuck inside. It helps to have online projects on rainy afternoons so that you can still feel productive.

In towns too small for your cell phone service provider to justify installing a cell tower, libraries can be your link to the outside world. Even if they're closed – and small-town libraries usually have minimal hours – you can still park out front and tap into their wireless network for as long as you need to upload photos and maintain your internet celebrity status.

Smartphone Apps

Smartphone apps are always evolving, and although many will fail to function on the backwoods roadways frequented by renegade travelers, a few select pieces of software on your device can ease the journey tremendously. Some apps work well even without a signal. The most useful tend to fit into the categories of Navigation, Campsites, Weather and Survival Skills.

Everyone's familiar with **Google Maps** and **MacOS Maps** for navigation, though few are aware that these programs can download maps ahead of time so that they can function offline via GPS when cell signals are sparse. **Maps.me** focuses primarily on its offline map capabilities. You type in your destination, and the app tells you how many map files you need to download in order to cover the terrain. It's effective, but the app takes some time to process through its data to plot out the driving route.

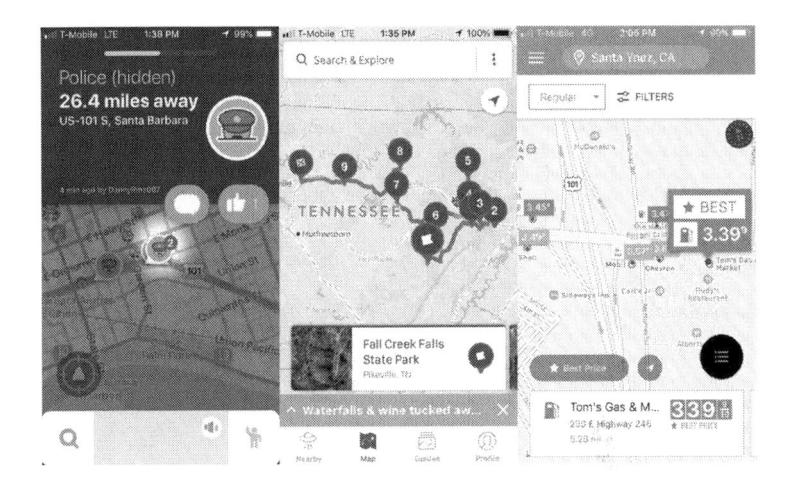

Waze is another popular navigation app that uses crowdsourced data to alert drivers of road hazards, such as wrecks, traffic bottlenecks and police cars, rerouting the driver when necessary. It loses its community advantage over other navigation programs in rural areas with few users, but it has a great feature in that you can add your friends and keep track of multiple vehicles when caravanning on a road trip. Just be aware that GPS-utilizing apps will drain your battery pretty quickly, so keep your phone plugged into the charger while driving.

Roadtrippers is a fun app for trip-planning. Search and select a bunch of destinations, and the app plots the best map for covering all that territory. It tells you the fuel cost, mileage and driving time. You can save trip itineraries, and it's easy to add additional destinations. One of the best features is its crowdsourced database of off-the-beaten-path locations.

And while you're driving around, use **Gasbuddy** to find the cheapest fuel near you. **GasGuru** does the same function but highlights the best price on the map for easier reference.

When you're looking for a renegade campsite, **Freecampsites.net** has a basic companion smartphone app for Android devices. If you're an iOS user, I recommend these alternatives: **Campendium** allows you to browse maps for free campsites and paid campgrounds. **BoonDocking** is more tailored to the RV enthusiast but limits itself to free sites and pull-outs. **iOverlander** remains my favorite – an app that allows you to search maps for renegade campsites, then open those locations in Google Maps or Maps.me to help you navigate there. Its best feature is the visitor update section for each location that tells you about the current campsite and road conditions.

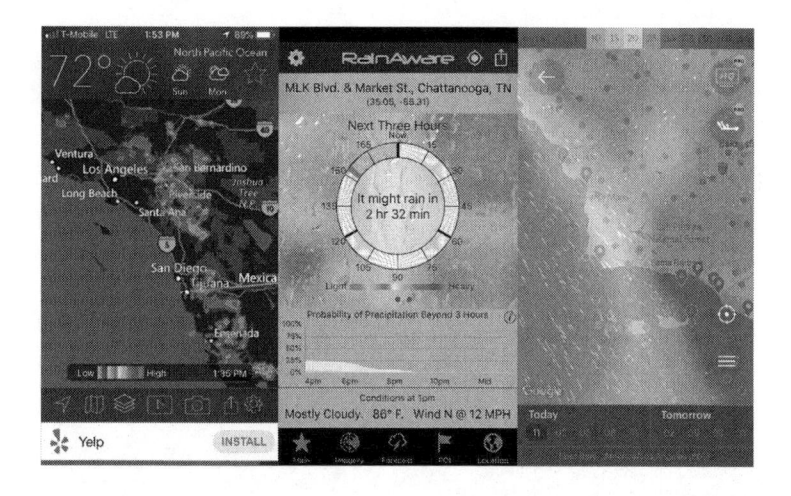

Numerous weather forecast apps exist out there, including the ones pre-installed into your smartphone and those that have interesting visual representations of predicted weather, like **Wunderground**. If you're good at interpreting radar maps, download **MyRadar**, which displays local radar units and updates every few minutes. For more immediate, hyperlocal weather predictions, consider paying a few bucks to try **RainAware** or **Dark Sky**. These apps sift through data to tell you precisely how many minutes from now that a rainstorm will strike your position.

And when you're considering pitching your tent atop a bluff for the most dramatic views, you might first want to consult **Windy**, which gives a simple representation of current airspeeds overlaid across a map of your area. You can also have it show you predicted windspeeds up to ten days in the future.

If you decide things are *really* going to get bad out there, or that the zombie apocalypse is imminent, you might want to install the **SurvivalGuide** app onto your phone. It's a free and thorough handbook, based on the U.S. Military Survival Manual, that covers shelter construction, water purification, firecraft, medicinal plants, dangerous animals and survival techniques that you can use in multiple habitats and weather conditions. Even if the world is not about to end, the appendix on knot-tying can be useful around your campsite or when securing equipment to the roof of your vehicle. Just try not to focus too hard on the chapter that covers Field-Expedient Weaponry. Remember, we're all friends here, trying to enjoy this beautiful country in a way that is harmonious, sustainable and leaves the renegade path open for future generations.

EPILOGUE: THE ROAD GOES EVER ON

So, we've come to the end of this guidebook and to the beginning of your journey into the vast landscapes of North America. It's time to unfold your maps, lay them out on the table and start scheming about the adventures to come. Charlie and I need to hit the road ourselves and check out some neglected corners of the country.

I hope that in these pages we have broadened your mind about the opportunities available to the renegade camper. Soon enough, you'll discover new strategies that are better tailored to your own vehicle, temperament and outdoor interests. For example, I once ran into a traveling family circus that would stay at state park campgrounds and create their own hot tub by connecting a hose from the bathroom's hot water spigot to an inflatable kiddie pool. Be creative, and don't resign yourself to discomfort while camping.

You can ask questions or share your own tips about life on the road by contacting me through *www.facebook.com/offthemapbooks* or *www.offthemapbooks.com/contact*. I would love to test out your strategies and incorporate them into future editions of this guidebook.

And now the open road awaits you. Where will you go? To the white gypsum sand dunes of New Mexico, perhaps? To the edge of the Grand Canyon, and into the twisted redrock ravines of Utah? Will you make your way through lightning-scarred summits to the ghost towns of the Colorado Rockies? Or fulfill a dream of witnessing the aurora borealis above the Arctic Circle? Go where your inspiration leads you, and do not fear the dead ends or detours that may arise. When considering the route ahead, a true renegade does not accept no for an answer. We *will*, however, accept a *maybe*... and then improvise like hell when we get there.

Safe travels!

LINKS

note: the author was not paid or compensated for any endorsements

Part One

- National Forest Service - www.fs.fed.us
- National Park Service – www.nps.gov
- Bureau of Land Management – www.blm.gov
- National Wildlife Refuge System - www.fws.gov/refuges
- Federal Recreation Website – www.recreation.gov

Part Two

- Marjorie Gersh-Young - <u>Hot Springs & Hot Pools of the Northwest</u>, <u>Hot Springs & Hot Pools of the Southwest</u>
- NOAA's Hot Springs Map – maps.ngdc.noaa.gov/viewers/hot_springs

Part Three

- Bob Wells - <u>How to Live in a Car, Van or RV: And Get Out of Debt, Travel, and Find True Freedom</u>
- Luci® Inflatable Solar Light - www.mpowerd.com
- WhisperLite™ Stove - www.msrgear.com/shop/stoves
- Jump Starting - www.wikihow.com/Jump-Start-a-Car, www.wikihow.com/Push-Start-a-Car
- Leave No Trace Principles – www.lnt.org

Part Four

- Couchsurfing – www.couchsurfing.com
- Hostelling International - www.hihostels.com
- Independent Hostels - www.hostelworld.com, www.hostelbookers.com
- AirBnB and Hipcamp – www.airbnb.com, www.hipcamp.com
- Craigslist Rideshare – www.craigslist.org
- Camping Recipes - www.backpackingchef.com, www.adventurediningguide.com, www.food.com/topic/camping
- Don Wright - Guide to Free Campgrounds: Includes Campgrounds $12 and Under in the United States
- Campsite Database – www.freecampsites.net
- Climbing Route Research - www.peakbagger.com, www.summitpost.org
- Smartphone Apps - www.google.com/maps, www.maps.me, www.waze.com, www.roadtrippers.com, www.gasbuddy.com, www.campendium.com, www.ioverlander.com, www.wunderground.com, www.myradar.com, www.rainaware.com, www.darksky.net

Epilogue

- Author Contact: www.facebook.com/offthemapbooks, www.offthemapbooks.com/contact

CAR CAMPING EQUIPMENT CHECKLIST

Vehicle

- spare key in magnetic case
- spare tire + jack
- tire repair kit or aerosol puncture sealant + 12-volt air compressor
- jumper cables
- jump starter power pack
- 12-volt car battery voltage monitor/USB charger
- folding shovel
- reflective windshield sun visor
- maps + guidebooks

Shelter

- tent + footprint
- stakes + mallet or hatchet
- inflatable mattress
- mattress inflator (12-volt or battery)
- insulation pad
- pillow + bedsheets
- sleeping bag and/or comforter
- tarp
- rope (parachute cord)

Kitchen

- 5-gallon water container

- water filter or purifying tablets
- camp stove + fuel + lighter
- pot + pan + plate + bowl + cup + utensils
- spatula + can opener + spices
- biodegradable napkins
- camp table

Campsite

- camp chair
- stadium chair
- solar lantern
- headlamp + batteries
- trash bags
- rags
- toilet paper + trowel + hand sanitizer
- warm clothes and raingear
- solar shower or pressure shower + washcloth + towel
- first aid kit
- insect repellent

ABOUT THE AUTHOR

Bryan Snyder grew up exploring the rolling hills and shady creeks of upstate New York. After college, he taught natural science to young students at various outdoor schools from Maine to Hawaii before settling on the West Coast.

His outdoor adventure column "Off The Map" was printed in Chenango County, New York's *The Evening Sun*. Additional photos and contact information may be found at *www.offthemapbooks.com*.

Bryan currently resides in the Santa Ynez Valley of California.

ABOUT THE VEHICLE

Charlie rolled off the assembly lines of Toledo, Ohio in 1994 and endured several years of salted winter highways in the Northeast before discovering a renewed sense of purpose on the backcountry roads of the Rocky Mountains.

Despite several accidents involving his engine mounts, he has recovered admirably and continues to assist collaborator Bryan Snyder in his travels.

Charlie is a Jeep Cherokee with over 400,000 miles. He has no plans to retire anytime soon.

A LIFELINE FOR THE RENEGADE TRAVELER

Need a little help finding renegade campsites?

Inside this short guidebook, you'll discover ten of the best options for your first forays into cross-country car camping, all chosen for their accessibility, natural beauty and capacity to handle the extra attention. Whether you're on the doorstep of Yellowstone Park or heading to Death Valley, these selections will help you begin your travels with success and confidence.

Best of all, both the guidebook and the camping are free. Pick up *Ten Renegade Camping Destinations* and start planning your journey today!

www.offthemapbooks.com/freebook

THE ADVENTURES BEGIN

OFF THE MAP
FIFTY-FIVE WEEKS OF ADVENTURING IN THE GREAT AMERICAN WILDERNESS AND BEYOND

BRYAN SNYDER

You've read the manual... now see what happens when you take Renegade Camping to the extreme!

Off The Map is a collection of fifty-five outdoor adventures that take place along the rougher and more precarious edges of our country's natural splendor. Within these stories, the author engages in ill-advised confrontations with the bears of Montana's Bob Marshall Wilderness, the mosquitoes of Yellowstone, and the voracious marmots of the San Juan Mountains. If you enjoy tales of haunted hotels and hot springs, hypothermia and heat exhaustion, as well as snapshots of the most scenic locations this continent has to offer, *Off The Map* will satisfy your inquisitive and adventurous spirit.

THE ADVENTURES CONTINUE

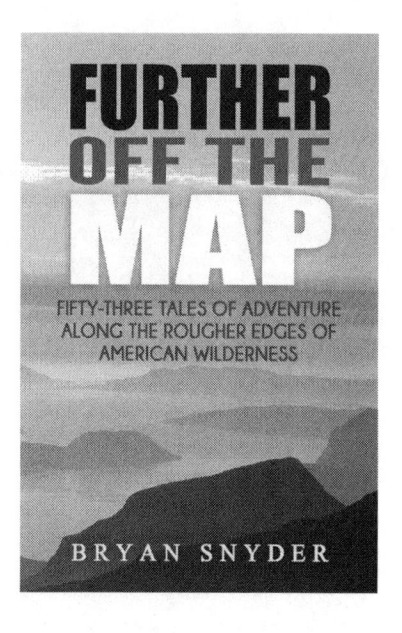

FURTHER OFF THE MAP

FIFTY-THREE TALES OF ADVENTURE ALONG THE ROUGHER EDGES OF AMERICAN WILDERNESS

BRYAN SNYDER

Further Off The Map invites you on a journey into the wild and inhospitable reaches of our continent in search of natural wonders both breathtaking and obscure. Join the author as he faces off against rattlesnakes, lightning bolts, dust storms and his own better judgment in the course of fifty-three misguided adventures – tales that span from the colossal volcanic peaks of the Pacific Northwest to the moonlit depths of the Grand Canyon.

With detours into the pyrotechnic metropolis of Burning Man and the hippie utopia of the Rainbow Gathering, this book celebrates the unique qualities of the American West, punctuated with humor, insight, and the risk of severe bodily injury.

THE ADVENTURES REACH THEIR CLIMAX

FALLING OFF THE MAP

FIFTY-FOUR EXPLORATIONS INTO THE WILDEST REACHES OF THE AMERICAN WEST

BRYAN SNYDER

Falling Off The Map draws you into a world of danger and wild beauty, weaving tales of majesty and misfortune, from sea level along the Lost Coast of California to the dizzying heights of Rainier's 14,441 feet. Follow the author as he dodges hailstorms in the Colorado Rockies, bushwhacks through the poison oak-infested hills of Big Sur, tracks grizzlies in the Beartooth-Absaroka Wilderness and sleds down the mighty volcanoes of the Pacific Northwest.

Featuring guest appearances by aggressive marmots, rebellious cows and the world's hungriest mosquitoes, this book highlights the plights, predicaments and precarious pleasures that can be found past the outposts of Western civilization. Pack a bag and join the adventure!

The Ghost and the Greyhound

BRYAN SNYDER
SUMMERDAY SAGA ~ BOOK ONE

The biggest secret in Earth's history is that *everything* is intelligent. Humans, animals, plants... even the deceased. Ancient magic kept the species from talking to one another... until one dog suddenly spoke up and asked his owner to help save the world.

Any other kid would have been thrilled to have a talking greyhound as a pet or to be recruited by a dead girl to stop an abomination from devouring the souls of his city. But thirteen-year-old Piers Davies of Summerday had bullies to avoid, a mother to take care of and a thousand other reasons to stay out of trouble. Nevertheless, the teenager soon found himself neck-deep in fairies, ghosts and bickering animals, most of whom considered him the sole ambassador of a species previously unknown for their intelligence - *the humans*.

The Summerday Saga starts here!

Made in the USA
Middletown, DE
18 July 2024